WHAT PEOPLE ARE SAYING ABOUT
**Suffering: if God exists, why doesn't he stop it?**

*I found this little book wonderf···· concise, free from religious jargon and v··· king. John Morris's and my ···· nt than might be expect··· ·nist for 20 years. Had I r···· clung on to faith for a wh···· ···wn me that DNA is full of design ···· ···uonal accidents waiting to happen'. Genetics get in the way of my agreeing with Morris's evolutionary position completely. Heritability studies suggest that our genetic lottery not only determines who gets genetic disease but also affects our ability to adapt and cope with it. Morris partly agrees, but finds room for God's supporting role in nature and human choices.*
**Dr Alison M Dunning,** Centre for Cancer Genetic Epidemiology, University of Cambridge

*How is it that some intelligent people go on trusting and hoping in God despite the challenges of science and, above all, suffering? I recommend as particularly suitable for group discussion this brief and helpful distillation of the ordinary wisdom about life, the universe and everything which has enabled people to sustain such faith.*
**Frances Young, OBE,** Emeritus Professor of Theology, University of Birmingham, mother of Arthur, born severely disabled, as in *Arthur's Call*

*Over 50 years I must have arranged about 30,000 funerals, some after significant suffering, and last year I went to Auschwitz. I have read this book twice and found it remarkable for its in-depth study. It very lucidly put each topic and each side of the debate and refers deferentially to other religions. It was a fascinating insight into the author's thoughts and I found myself questioning my own. Many of our bereaved families would find comfort from this book and help them realise they are not alone in their suffering.*

**Richard Steel,** Richard Steel & Partners, Funeral Directors since 1860

*John Morris offers a valuable insight into the paradox that must trouble every believer. His family experience drives him to better understand this question and this brings a deep humanity. His writing is concise, accessible and enlightening, both for people whose faith is tested and for those of us who may not be believers but seek to better understand those who are. A stimulating and well crafted read.*

**Mark Goldring,** Chief Executive, Oxfam GB; formerly Chief Executive, Mencap

*For clarity, brevity, readability and comprehensiveness, this book, on a vexed topic, is one of the very best. It is open to insights from the sciences and the world's religions, as well as those from theology and faith. Ideal for discussion in groups or for private reading, perhaps in a single session, it handles deep problems with a light touch. It will be of great*

*help to believers and agnostics alike.*
**Professor Adrian Thatcher,** Dept of Theology and Religion, University of Exeter

*This book contains so much wisdom packed into so few pages. It is condensed from the author's deep understanding of suffering and is both scientifically and theologically well reasoned. It is an excellent and remarkable book. Inspired !*
**Sir Colin Humphreys, CBE, FRS,** Director of Research, Dept of Materials Science and Metallurgy, University of Cambridge

# Suffering:

## if God exists,
## why doesn't he stop it?

# Suffering:
## if God exists,
## why doesn't he stop it?

John Morris

www.contemporarycreed.org.uk

Winchester, UK
Washington, USA

First published by Circle Books, 2016
Circle Books is an imprint of John Hunt Publishing Ltd., Laurel House,
Station Approach, Alresford, Hants, SO24 9JH, UK
office1@jhpbooks.net
www.johnhuntpublishing.com
www.circle-books.com

For distributor details and how to order please visit the 'Ordering' section on
our website.

Text copyright: John Morris 2015

ISBN: 978 1 78535 011 5
Library of Congress Control Number: 2015950689

A CIP catalogue record for this book is available from the British Library.

Design: Stuart Davies

Printed in the USA by Edwards Brothers Malloy

We operate a distinctive and ethical publishing philosophy in
all areas of our business, from our global network of authors
to production and worldwide distribution.

# CONTENTS

Suffering: if God exists, why doesn't he stop it?

Other books by John Morris

***Contemporary Creed***: *a mini-course in Christianity for today.*

O-Books 2005

*Revised edition:* ***Contemporary Creed***: *Reasonable pathways*
*through the problems of Christian beliefs and ethics.*

O-Books 2012

# Foreword by the Archbishop of York

The question as to how a loving God can permit suffering is pertinent in every generation and language. This book provides a step by step approach to the issue of human suffering. It will help anyone seeking to understand the reality of pain, loss, and evil, in the context of faith in a loving God.

In my experience it is often those who have encountered searing grief who offer the best help with this question. This book is evidence of that. True to form, John Morris, my inspiring former teacher of English, has been rigorous in his enquiry, drawing the insights of philosophy, theology, and contemporary science in constructing a robust intellectual response.

For me, it is Jesus who offers the surest hope that God, who is love, has not made a mistake in creating this world. In the life, death, and resurrection of Jesus we see God's new creation breaking in, the future invading the present, opening up new possibilities, and new purposes. John Morris shows us how it is in Christ, that we find the way through this 'vale of tears' to transforming faith, hope, and love.

For all who wrestle with this question, this is a 'must read!'

**+Sentamu Eboracensis**

# Acknowledgements

My life has been a continuous education, picking up other people's ideas, and using some of them here, hopefully freshly expressed. Only parts of the book are original. Grief has taught me too, though I have been fortunate compared with what many millions have to endure.

I am indebted to those who have read and commented on earlier drafts, including Revd Dr John Polkinghorne, FRS, Dr David Girling, Abdul-Azim Ahmed (*On Religion* editor), Jenny Nockolds, and especially Dr Alison Dunning for expert help with genetics. Keith Williams has helped with computer drafts and my publisher, John Hunt, has again backed me.

My best critic has been Mary, my wife since 1960, who has patiently read all versions and offered many improvements. Any remaining errors are my own!

But my greatest thanks are to Amanda, and her loyal husband Ashley, for my grandson Daniel, who is my best teacher and friend; and for allowing him to stay with Mary and me at regular intervals; and for permission to mention him a little in the text.

## Dedication

To all who suffer and all who care, including Heshron Rahmi, Principal in Kalimpong, Darjeeling (www.albellaboyshome.co.uk) and my grandchildren, Oliver, Lucy, James, Alistair, and Alexander, who also care for Daniel.


## Royalties

To Equipment for Disabled Children
(www.e4dc.org.uk)

# Preface

In 2012 my revised *Contemporary Creed* (CC) was published. It was intended as an A-Z, subtitled *Reasonable pathways through the problems of Christian beliefs and ethics.* Unsurprisingly, the problem of suffering was one of its themes. In 2013, while leading a Science and Faith week at Lee Abbey in Devon, fresh ways of expressing the subject began to crystallise. So now it is time to revise and expand on previous ideas.

Other books on suffering are often long on biography, with inspiring examples of how individuals have responded to personal disaster, but short on what interests me most - *the big picture.* Are there *global* explanations of how suffering can be compatible with the existence of God, especially a Christian God of Love? Writers often blame the Devil, and Adam and Eve, for wrecking a good world. Certainly human sin greatly exacerbates the problem but additional explanations are needed to be true to modern science and everyday reality.

Brevity is my preferred style, which will be no surprise to anyone reading my short creed in *CC* (1). It can all be read at www.contemporarycreed.org.uk. That creed, in everyday language, squeezed the essence of the book's 208 pages into a nutshell of just 100 words! My new challenge is to summarise the ever-present problem of suffering, about which so much has been written over the centuries, into a brief paperback, while not skating over the difficulties. So here is a '100 minutes read', while relaxing over a drink or two! By reading it all in one go, you will more easily see the ideas in my chain of argument hang together, like links in a necklace chain. That speed means more people are likely to read it, or discuss it in groups, and hopefully find it of some help. Again, I will donate the royalties to charity.

My goal is not only to answer my title, *Suffering: if God exists, why doesn't he stop it?* but along the way to answer a related second question *Suffering: is this God's best possible world?* This second one was the title of my article, published in edited form, in the magazine *On Religion*, Issue 8, autumn 2014, pp30, 31, and some of its ideas are now here.

May I invite you to email me with your own better ideas or frank criticism, so that I can learn from you?

John Morris, Winchester, UK, 2015.

# Where is God?

"Where is God and what is he doing?" was Goethe's question on hearing news of the 1755 Lisbon earthquake. It speaks for all of us when innocent children die, nations starve, cities are bombed, and we attend funerals. It expresses the ancient problem of suffering which has always been the weakest pillar holding up all religions, and the strongest ground for atheism. Without God, there is no religious problem: suffering is 'simply' part of life's double package of joy and woe, that I witnessed during my nine years on the equator in Uganda.

While helping to care for my own grandson born in 1999 profoundly handicapped - and Daniel is still unable to crawl, walk, talk, and has to be fed and changed - I wrote my *Contemporary Creed* (CC) which expands on points I shall refer to only briefly here. Those born without a chance of a week of 'normal' life, and beyond medical repair, raise bigger questions about God's world than calamities to healthy bodies.

Can one square the circle and solve the apparent contradiction between suffering and a loving God? I shall try to show it is reasonable to cling on to belief, when one's hands are slipping on the rope over a cliff edge, facing one of life's horrors.

# A definition of the problem of suffering

The perennial problem of suffering can be summarised in a nutshell: "If the Creator is good, a kind father to his creatures, he cannot be almighty in a world of abundant suffering. But if he is almighty, he cannot also be good because he lets suffering continue. Therefore God lacks goodness or power or both. But a God who is deficient in goodness or power is not what people call God: therefore he does not exist" (2).

Thus the atheist wins by a neat knockdown argument! I wish my comeback below could be equally swift, but no reader would be convinced by a few Twitter messages! So please stay with me as I try to be as brief as this complex subject allows. The first few sections - which are not conventional chapters but simply steps in an argument - are often very short so you may find yourself galloping through the pages!

# Scientific progress and wrong answers to suffering

The word 'optimism' is associated in dictionaries with Leibniz (1646-1716) who, though surrounded by natural disasters and human evil, remained optimistic. His God was not an under-achiever but the Creator of "the best of all possible worlds"; a phrase he felt had roots in Plato. With modern progress in science we are in a better position to discuss whether the Earth is the Creator's best habitat for today's humans or their only possible environment.

My discussion depends on readers being open-minded about my first assumption below, from which follows a sequence of steps in the argument that sometimes pretend more knowledge of God than humans possess! His mysterious transcendence was well expressed by a Jewish prophet: "My thoughts are not your thoughts, nor are your ways my ways" (3). I try hard to avoid *inappropriately* human (anthropomorphic) language in describing God but I do not always succeed! So those thoughts must remain tentative.

First a health warning, in order to avoid misunderstanding. I do *not* mean "all is for the best" in a cot death, blindness, or cancer. I am *not* saying: "God has everything under control"; "God allowed, willed or planned it"; "We all die in God's good time"; "God

wanted mummy in heaven and has a reason for everything"; "The unfortunate exist to make the rest of us
kinder"; "It was all Adam's fault for ruining a perfect
world"; "This is God's punishment on our wrongdoing
or lack of faith in order to make us better people".
These quotes are, I suggest, inappropriate responses to
*particular individual* circumstances.

Another common response is to give up, saying
"We don't know and never will, because God's ways
are beyond us humans". But I hope what follows will
show that we do know more than we think.

More appropriate responses will emerge as we
examine the whole *global system.* In that big picture we
shall discover if there is any justification for saying
about suffering that "God allowed, willed or planned
it".

To find an answer we need evidence of how the
world behaves, and this scientific method weighs
particular events and human experience before it
makes broad generalisations. With my family
background, I value the realism of this bottom-up
thinking, more than top-down airy-fairy dogma - what
matters is whether God-talk is true to life! But my book
title requires a combination of both approaches: "if
God exists, why doesn't he stop" suffering? We first
need to agree on what the word 'God' means - he has
many varieties! - and then discuss what sort of God
there could be to make this sort of world.

# Does God exist?

Not in Richard Dawkins' best seller *The God Delusion*. But the God he dismissed was often too small to be the real God. So may I ask my atheist readers "Which God do you not believe in?" because I too reject false ideas. My CC weighs the clues - not *proofs* - in modern science, nature and morality that hint of a Creator of supreme intelligence, based on arguments from design, first cause, rationality, order, beauty, coherence, and - above all for me - the amazing fine tuning of the universe.

I shall not repeat those clues here. Nor shall I use the American phrase 'intelligent design'. I am very aware that against design might be set mal-design; against moral order, random suffering for all creatures.

There is at least one big issue we all face. Not 'God or evolution?' because, unlike Dawkins, one can accept both God *and* evolution. Not 'Who caused God?' for that reduces the nature of infinite God, the uncaused cause. 'God or chance?' - yes, that is our choice. I have intelligent friends who opt for chance, a lucky cosmic accident, to explain what exists. That is their huge faith which I respect. Is faith in God as big a leap into the unknown?

# My first assumption

To try to make sense of suffering, I start with only one clue to God's existence, namely what is called the ontological argument. Reworking St Anselm (1033-1109), my premise is that God is the greatest idea that the human mind can imagine.

But an idea of something does not prove its existence. If God is a theoretical concept without existence, there is something lacking: real existence seems necessary to complete the truth of that supreme idea. I assume God's objective existence to be eternal, unlimited by space-time, and immaterial Spirit. This One Being is without gender, though for convenience I refer to God as he, rather than writing each time he/she/it.

My first assumption is not self-evidently true, especially if the word 'God' is spoiled by bad memories of a violent father-figure, barren churchgoing, or temple idols. So my premise is an acceptable foundation only if I build on it the highest quality of God, the summit of which means he is both personal and loving. To readers who find no evidence of a kind God, I admit that part of me agrees with them! With one eye I see only my family experience, world conflicts, and savage nature.

My one-eyed thinking sees no ambiguities, just evidence pointing all one way, against God. But my

two-eyed thinking is more balanced and sees contradic-
tions that prompt me to dig deeper into his puzzling
world.

# A Good God of Holy Love

That greatest idea means God is Good. He did not create that goodness; it is his eternal nature or character. That good essence always seeks to propagate Good - though too literal a reading of parts of the Bible might reach less favourable conclusions!

Too much can be made by some philosophers of the intractable problem of defining Good, when most of us know what it means for everyday use. God wills something because *he* is good. If that is true, it follows that something is right because he wills it. (To say God wills something because the thing is good makes him subservient to good.)

Nature red in tooth and claw might suggest an evil First Cause. I've sometimes thought the same when face to face with the suffering of African children and loved ones in pain: if God exists, where is his mercy? Yet such dark thoughts belittle the splendour of God as the greatest idea, the superlative concept, especially when balanced by the wonder, beauty and pleasure in the natural world. Even those who condemn the Creator's inhumanity, choose to bring babies into the world, on the grounds presumably that life is precious, a gift worth handing on.

The greatest Good is ethical perfection, very different from human imperfections and wrongdoing.

13

That moral excellence or Holiness sets God apart from his creation and its creatures, in awesome Otherness, so he delights in good and opposes evil (4). A Good Creator is the highest *Pure* Love, not self-centred, dominating and fluctuating, but constantly outgoing, unconditional kindness and compassion, a personal quality in God who is personal but *not a human person*.

The essence of love is to will and do the best for the beloved - and *at the same time for all the beloved*, in so far as that is possible. For mortals that universal and timeless activity is not possible: human love, whether affection, friendship, passion, or God-like charity, is limited. Whereas the greatest God would have an all-embracing desire to do what is best always for every-thing and everyone. As far as we can judge, that involves compromise between competing claims upon his love.

# The Almighty - in what way is God omnipotent?

An impotent God would not amount to the greatest idea. That highest conception requires him to be omnipotent and rational which includes firstly, the power to create something other than itself, a *material* universe or multiverse, with laws and order, reflecting his own rationality.

Secondly, the power to restrict himself, if and when he chooses. Before our universe began, mathematical physical laws were presumably in the Creator's mind, which he then chose to use as the framework for an unfolding creation, thereby imposing limits to the use of his power. Since that beginning, the Creator's original choice seems to have been continually confirmed, down the ages. Rarely, it seems, from the evidence humans have, does he lift a self-imposed restriction to intervene and overrule as an Almighty God could do.

A continually Controlling God, is not necessarily the greatest idea or the greatest Love. On the other hand a God who has *permanently* surrendered or lost all control and *never* wishes to resume benevolent rule is not what we would expect of the greatest God, who is both the beginning and end, the first and last, the Ultimate.

# Cosmology

In so far as I understand it, cosmology suggests to me that an evolutionary process was the only choice open to God consistent with his purpose. A small, young creation would be no good to us. Only a big universe is an old universe, lasting the billions of years needed to produce stars, heavier elements, carbon-based life, and eventually us, a vastly more ingenious continuous creation than one in a flash. Instead of finished species, primitive forms acquired the capacity for wonderful self-development and adaptation.

A detailed inflexible plan from beginning to end would allow no freedom to God or his creatures. If intelligent humans were an intended objective as the anthropic principle suggests, the omnipotent Creator had ironically no choice but to create slowly by stellar, chemical, and biological evolution. No short cuts, only the gradualism of emergent creation. Thereby Mind could eventually express love to other minds dependent on carbon formed only inside stars.

# God the Discoverer

The greatest idea that the human mind can imagine does not have to be a static concept of eternal change-lessness. Instead of a God with an initial blueprint of the universe mapping out every step, I wrote about God as the great Discoverer of where creation leads. I later discovered that early Muslim scientists had much the same thought!

"Let us make humankind in our image" (5) pictures God on an adventure to multiply goodness, who would later discover in Jesus what humankind is like from the inside. The greatest all-knowing God knows and foresees only *all that is possible,* so he cannot know or predict the *precise* future until it exists - or who will win Wimbledon or next week's lottery! The soccer crowd hymn "Change and decay in all around I see/ O Thou who changest not/ Abide with me" expresses great feeling but less understanding of inventive God, prepared to experiment and take risks, in search of greater Good of overall benefit.

For us mortals, time always flows in one direction, linear, from beginning to end. The eternal God that I attempt to describe is both outside time and making real discoveries within a creation that is genuinely emerging. He is not one for whom cosmic history (past, present and future) is a film already viewed, as if time could be seen in two directions, forwards and backwards.

# The Big Bang and inherent violence

In Genesis, most long 'geological days' end with "God saw that it was good" - not perfect, but fit for purpose. Perhaps God rested on the seventh to let his six 'ingredients' take their course. Since the Big Bang 13.7 billion years ago, the Creator *appears* to observe a continuous Sabbath rest, letting creation make itself through *seemingly* undirected evolution. That remorseless process involves the mathematical laws of nature appearing to operate as a self-governing rational system in which - for non-religious scientists like Stephen Hawking and Martin Rees - God is unnecessary to trigger our violent universe, and certainly not needed to sustain the process once started (6).

That violence - on which we depend, warmed by the sun's explosiveness - was not introduced by legendary Adam's sin, for humans are a relatively recent arrival. Nor, in my view, was it introduced by the Evil One, variously described as a fallen angel, Satan, the serpent, or the Devil, leaving God himself blameless. Surely, the heavenly existence of a powerful adversary would diminish the idea of the one and only greatest God. Yet our ancestors battled with opposites, alternating daylight and darkness, health and sickness, harvests and famine. We too see a chasm between the ideal and the actual; after 'wars to end all wars', conflicts continue, catastrophes fill our TV, and some viewers might wonder if a sort of evil impulse or demonic force is at work besides individual misbehaviour.

Talk of the Devil is more of a joke to both the atheist and deist. Deism is the belief in an impersonal Creator who, after setting the ball rolling, has taken his hands off and ignores what follows, taking no side in any conflict between good and evil. Whether Einstein was amongst those scientists who are deists is debatable (7). Other scientists, notably John Polkinghorne, go further, thinking that some of the mystery in our universe has been removed by God's revelation of himself (8). Their theism and my own is a faith in a double agency, God and natural forces: a restless Creator, constantly interacting, rather than sometimes intervening from outside, with the unfolding and open process he began and upholds, rich in its alternative possibilities.

If God is not a necessary being, one can still argue that he is a rational hypothesis. It may look as though the universe is making itself, yet it is reasonable to believe that nature and its *beings* exist and are kept *in being* through the only One with *Being in itself*, the original essence and sustainer of *all being*, the perpetual *I am*.

But is that Quintessential Consciousness aware of human suffering? He would need to be to want to stop it. The Deist God is so far removed from his creation, that he would be either unaware of or unmoved by its pain. The Qur'an - to be considered later - occasionally implies that Allah is so different from us and completely self-sufficient, that he is unaffected by the actions of his transient creatures. Certainly, Michelangelo's finger gap between the Creator and his creatures is an important truth. Yet two other monotheistic faiths, Judaism and Christianity, take the astonishing jump of faith to a God *who is deeply affected* by human behaviour, and responds to it. Without that faith, my Discoverer God would not possess the *personal* qualities and nature I have given him.

I have said this personal God "responds to it". But how? The greatest personal God chooses influence rather than force, guidance rather than manipulation. We shall go on to see (p49) that this Influential God does not *send disasters on purpose* as an opportunity to win his way, but uses whatever happens as an invitation to move on, with his help, to turn what looks permanent pitch-black night into at least a hint of dawn.

# Freedom and creativity are both indivisible

Humans are stardust: they cannot be given moral freedom without material freedom being given to their constituent particles. Subatomic particles in the quantum world have an unpredictability, indeterminacy, within the overall cosmic order (9). Particles, bacteria, and animals behave 'freely' in the painful and *amoral* natural world - without moral choice to act otherwise; savage predation, parasitism, and the food chain all contribute to the survival of the fittest and 'best'. But higher up the evolutionary ladder, human animals are aware of moral choices between right and wrong.

Freewill versus determinism is an ongoing debate: some neuroscientists think freewill, the self, and the brain-mind duality are illusions and humans are entirely chemical machines. Certainly, genes do determine your height and looks - and my unlucky baldness! Genes *influence* behaviour but do not *determine* it and delete all personal responsibility. It is too reductionist to turn humans into mechanisms, as if puppets pulled by their gene strings, or motor homes for gene drivers! There is more truth in what some doctors say, "Nature loads the gun and the environment pulls the trigger". No one has complete freedom, especially starving people, but there is a degree of discretion in the way people cope with appalling situations - and in a pedestrian's refusal to cross the road just in front of an advancing bus!

Like freedom, creativity is also indivisible. Inexhaustible creativity is not only a characteristic of the Creator; it is endowed in his image on the evolving natural world whose ingenuity for generating new forms and abilities is breathtaking. David Attenborough's superb collection of films demonstrates the point repeatedly. Though full of wonder, he cannot imagine any merciful Creator behind nature's mixture of delight and destruction.

There is no limit either in human creativity, not only in films and cameras. Endless human inventions and upgrading of the internet, smart phones, and space travel, make the future almost unimaginable! Transformational creativity has the potential to generate not only new physical structures but new ideas, and greater understanding of ourselves and the cosmos, thanks to our possession of what has developed into the most complex 'object' in the universe, the human brain and its mysteriously non-material and self-conscious mind, 'me'.

# Robots or free-thinking people?

The Creator of the *material* universe (or of the vibrating strings of energy that underlie all matter, as string theory suggests) is impotent to create *immaterial* good at the drop of a hat. Amoral, clockwork robots could have been programmed to be good, instantly; but that would be God's own goodness returned to him.

Might we imagine a self-sufficient God, who had no need of us, nevertheless thinking "If I could create autonomous moral beings, they could return something distinctively fresh?" Unlike a robot, each free-thinking person - however handicapped - could be unique: no one else would have quite the same thoughts, emotions, character and experience of the world. Such would be his dignity, his inviolable, even sacred worth. That special person, in return for God's love, could choose to offer his own special love in response.

But the gift of freedom is risky, as every parent knows. Love may be rejected, whether from parents or from a Servant God who waits expectantly, rather than controlling us as an Absolute Ruler. Archetypal Adam and Eve rebelled, showing Love's outcome is unpredictable and painful. The safe way for free-thinking people to avoid hurt, is to remain detached, never to fall in love, never to care deeply and give themselves to a cause or another's welfare. The freedom to love is the freedom to become vulnerable, to open ourselves to suffering (10).

# Costly virtues

Morality cannot be created or commanded into being in the Garden of Eden. "Let us make humankind in our image" expresses God's wish to grow godlikeness (godliness) in others. The highest virtues of selfless love and forgiveness, like others including generosity, courage, honesty, tolerance, trustworthiness, empathy, and endurance, cannot be ready-made. Values emerge only in the moral struggle of tough decisions in trying circumstances: for example, bravery cannot grow in comfort, but only in real danger.

To create morally responsible, independent beings, God has to allow real consequences to the good and evil we do. Were he to do everything for us and rescue us from each impending disaster, we would have smaller brains and remain immature children. *There is no way round it:* a loving parent-Father has to restrain himself and let his 'baby' of virtue climb onto its own two wobbly feet!

Yet behind the emergence of self-conscious humans, sieved by natural selection, was a providence that helped virtues to be born, initially as a survival mechanism, which graduated into altruism for *complete strangers*. Thus Love is a multiplier. Not only can people be the *receivers* of the love and virtues of God, they can become *givers*, God's agents freely choosing to spread his goodness without discrimination to friend and foe alike. From one source, the ripples of Love have, after billions of years, been detected and disseminated (11).

Sadly, we cannot have moral beauty without the beast: moral giants of forgiveness like Nelson Mandela breathed the same air as monsters like Hitler. In smaller ways we too are to blame for our contribution to man-made global warming, our carbon footprint from cars and planes, fossil fuels, deforestation to meet rising demand for meat, over-population, and selfish share of the world's resources. So not all natural disasters are the Creator's fault, what insurers call 'acts of God'!

Virtues in self-conscious humans may give us a 'transformation clue' – not proof – of the existence of God, whose creative process might be summed up in either of these two 'formulas':

(a) Personal Being  >  materialism  >  personalised materialism.

A Personal God (not person) creates impersonal matter, which he eventually transforms into personalised beings, who can imagine supreme personal qualities like love, justice, and forgiveness. Such seemingly timeless virtues suggest a spiritual reality, a world of values that co-exists with the material world, and reigns in judgement over it. This sovereignty of good survives independently, whether or not people live up to its ideals and admit to a lingering hunger for the absolute best.

(b) Mind > materialism > mindful materialism.

Mind gives birth to matter, from which mindful creatures emerge. A caterpillar to chrysalis to butterfly are remarkable changes of form (metamorphosis). Metabolism is the sum of chemical changes in living matter. Can we say that the most astonishing change came when God's process elevated materialism into spiritual beings, by 'metabolising' one body part, the brain, into *thinking flesh*, an inquiring god-like *mind*, able to imagine abstract ideas like 'good', 'myself', 'God' and 'infinity' ?

# Evolution's gains and losses

What does *not* have a plus and minus? Ambiguity is everywhere. *Everything has a price.* My process theology entails mistakes, extinctions, and waste, for luck, chance and accident are features of life. The evolution of life is driven by genetic mutation in cells. Without accidental mutations - which sometimes result in cancerous cells - we humans would not have arrived! Scientists have discovered that only a system with *both* order and disorder (including quantum uncertainties) delivers novelties that can survive.

Yet this creativity seems to result in less than 1% of babies being born with such severe genetic defects that not even a loving God could reverse. These babies, either at conception or in their development in the womb, never have a chance of 'normality', unlike children whose first years are fine until terminal illness strikes. All are unlucky casualties, but the 1% are especially the vicarious sufferers on behalf of the 99%. Without them who knows if a genetic axe might have fallen on your family - as it did on my own? In a crisis one's first thought might be "Why me?", but one's better second thought could be "Why not me?"

Ironically, mutations are extremely *useful* for genetic research and medical progress. *Random* mutations express the *orderly* structure of DNA molecules in all living matter: creativity is maximised through exploring the gamut of potentialities within ordered genetic sentences that randomly misspell, sometimes detrimentally, but sometimes beneficially in real novelty within particular environments.

As molecular biologists uncover the immense complexity of one cell amongst the trillions within the human body, is it not unreasonable to expect everyone to remain healthy, when so much could go wrong? Heart attacks and strokes happen, yet the high degree of healthy bodies is an amazing achievement. It is either nature's unaided triumph or God assists it and all medical progress. Proof either way is impossible, for we cannot experiment by taking God out of the equation to see if things work without him!

"But where was your God's compassion for many thousands of years before modern medicine arrived?" the sceptic rightly asks. Throughout history, all accumulating progress in science, engineering and technology has been a slow climb until its rapid acceleration in the modern era. God does not present things on a plate: he wants responsible persons to achieve great things through human hands and brains, as if to some extent masters of their own destiny. So we are the on-stage actors doing the work while he assists off-stage out of sight, allowing his own 'hands' to be tied by his good purpose.

# Ends and means

God's goal is to multiply Good, because he is Love, with the best intentions. The means he uses to achieve that end necessarily requires evolution, creativity and moral freedom, and they entail intrinsic suffering.

Olympic competitors know that without the coach's punishing training there will be no medals; this grinding method is the necessary price paid to reach the top. God, like their coach, does not have an evil purpose and want the suffering itself - were there another way he would take it - he wants victory in the race, *if* the world is his Olympic training ground of soul-making! So suffering is the *consequence* of the way everything has to be, it is the cost of Love that makes things free.

Terrible adversity may be ennobling, transforming sufferers and their carers into saints, heroes all of them but mostly unknown, never hitting the headlines like Stephen Sutton and Mulala. Stephen, the 19-year-old cancer victim who died in May 2014, raised over £5 million for the Teenage Cancer Trust charity, its greatest fundraiser. Who can forget his smiling thumbs up gesture from his bedside?

Malala Yousafzai, an activist from the age of 11, was shot in the head when 14 by Taliban gunmen, for campaigning for girls' education in Pakistan. Airlifted to Birmingham, UK, for urgent operations, she won the 2014 Nobel Peace Prize at 17, the youngest ever recipient.

But such inspiring heroism, that creatively converts calamity into something beautiful, does not make any suffering *good in itself*. Good may be its *outcome*, to the extent that some sufferers - unlike me - would even call their problem a *'blessing* in disguise'. Sadly, suffering can destroy the body, mind and spirit, and swamp the emotions, especially when sufferers find no meaning, only pointless pain. Crushed by events over which they have no control, victims can feel justifiable anger, resentment, bitterness, and self-pity. Some will become more convinced atheists, or lose whatever faith they had.

# Rough justice

Some suffering is our own fault whereas I guess that most is undeserved and unjust. Hindus and Buddhists believe people *ultimately* reap what they sow, from a moral law of cause and effect (*karma*). In an unforgiving cycle of births and deaths, this law of karma raises or lowers one's status in the next life by present good or bad deeds; it also implies that Indian society is fair because a person has only himself to blame for the inferior position he now occupies as a result of misdeeds in previous lives. But the scales of justice in this world are inevitably imperfect: it is unfair when criminals escape justice and their innocent victims suffer.

If karma's moral law is hard to prove, a health 'law' is easier: it demonstrates a causal link between cigarettes or drink driving and a premature death. But recent cancer research suggests that though lifestyle choices can greatly increase the risks to health, most cancers are caused by bad luck - if frequent cell divisions increase the chances of mutations that turn out harmful - rather than by other things also beyond our control, namely inherited genes or the environment (12).

Recognising bad luck and unfairness, the Bible sometimes promises a defence of the defenceless and justice for the righteous. But elsewhere there are less sweeping statements, so deeper interpretation is needed beyond the literal, balancing one text with another. God *wishes and does what he can* to bring justice and offer the psalmist's 'umbrella' to protect his persecuted people in the rain of arrows. But his global system places constraints on what can be delivered. To bypass or overrule his free human agencies might undermine his objective of all-round benefit.

Good and bad people live together so how could God be selective in a train crash, Ebola epidemic or flood? If prayers were always answered as we asked, or evil people were *always* punished and the innocent *always* protected and rewarded, that would be a less ethical world, not more. It would incline us to pray and be good for the reward rather than for its own sake! The self-interested gain/loss factor would poison motives and actions.

The Old Testament book of Job shows that the best religious beliefs are not reward-based. Satan tries to prove they are, by robbing Job of his wealth, his servants, his ten children, and his health. But instead of cursing God, and despite many unanswered questions, Job still manages to retain his unconditional belief in the Lord.

# A better world: (a) with less liberty

Freedom is indivisible, as we have already noted. There is either appropriate freedom for all creation or no freedom, it is all or nothing. Yet, who has not cried out "Why did God not intervene to stop the natural 'evil' of an earthquake, tsunami, or hurricane? Or correct the faulty chromosomes or genes? Or halt the cancer? Or stop the human evil of Holocaust killers and terrorist atrocities?" So we put God in the dock and declare him guilty of negligence, failing to be a troubleshooting God.

We regard freedom as a fundamental human right but sometimes we want God to limit the freedom of bacteria and that of a gunman, child abuser, or rapist when freedom runs riot. Yet have we thought through what we are asking from God? If he had done what I asked, am I prepared to take the consequences? Where could he draw the line to stop his interventions reducing *everyone's* and *everything's* liberty? He could easily see the line with tsunamis - no one wants them to hurt - but any intervention would have big consequences.

Governments too are torn between protecting freedom of speech, freedom of the press, a person's privacy, and freedom to migrate while at the same time drawing sensible boundaries. One man's freedom restricts another's. I might want intervention to stop my partner's betrayal – but a God that removes the 'right' and freedom to do 'evil', is bound also to remove the freedom to do good.

By definition, the freedom to choose means doing one thing, not another. But we prefer to have it both ways: to sleep around but keep our marriage; to ski or climb mountains but never to lose a leg; to fly but never to crash. As I said earlier "Everything has a price": we cannot enjoy everything at the same time, so we choose to gain one thing at the expense of another, and that choice brings risks and responsibilities. Especially *things of value* do not come cheaply, only at a price. The same must surely apply to God too.

To want a safe environment - so the sun warms but never causes skin cancer, with seas good for sailing but never dangerous - is to want the impossible. God's system has to combine lawful necessity and chance happenings. Volcanoes and tectonic plates are left free to be themselves, bringing, we now know, some beneficial scientific consequences as well as personal calamities. If God were unreliable, often overruling his physical laws and interrupting cause and effect, scientists would not know where they are. In short, life would become chaotic, defeating progress. A Safety Officer, at his cosmic radar screen diverting dangers, reduces the greatest God to an unpredictable Dictator, and shrinks adults to irresponsible children, relying entirely on parent-God to keep them safe!

# A better world: (b) with more comfort

Imagine two alternative worlds, one easy and one hard. The easy, comfortable world offers minimum pain and maximum pleasure from minimum effort. The hard world offers the potential to maximise values and make better people through maximum effort. Which would we choose?

The easy paradise has food and water for everyone, with no need to share limited resources; no pressure to work hard all week; and fewer injuries, hospitals, fire brigades, police forces, and armies. But in this easy world with few hardships and dangers, there would be less need for bravery, generosity, and self-sacrificing concern for others, so how would these virtues flourish? Whereas in the hard world these virtues would be much in demand so love, caring and forgiveness would have to grow and multiply. Demand and supply would operate.

It seems that God has chosen our present hard world as the best environment for the emergence of strong values and happier, more responsible people. So the good life was not meant to be easy but challenging. When in pain, the easy bland world may seem bliss, but it turns out to be inferior in value. Conversely, the tough stressful world has the best redemptive value. Not that God is a monster enforcing slogans like 'pain is good for you', or 'if it's not hurting it's not working'. Rather, it is human virtues that dictate what's required: they cannot develop except through moral struggle in often distressing situations that can make or sadly break us.

Research has shown that some of us break more easily than others due to variations in resilience - the ability to adapt and cope with disease and other stressful events. Resilience is in part learned and can be improved but a proportion is inherited from a combination of different genes. As with a card game, some of us inherit a strong hand and others a much weaker combination. We might conclude that such unequal inheritance proves God is unfair. But humans are generally healthier for having their genes mixed through intercourse, so how could God give equal shares without scrapping the pleasure and evolutionary benefit of sex? I can't imagine many hands up for that better world!

Genes work, not in isolation but together, and with the environment (which includes lifestyle and other personal choices, diet, living conditions, willpower, example, etc.). So genes may not be the only thing to praise or blame but a whole complex range of factors.

# A better world: (c) with flexible laws of physics

Regular and remorseless laws of nature are our lot, a given. For Einstein the "most incomprehensible thing about the universe is that it is comprehensible"; rational maths was built in from the beginning and we, billions of years later, discover it. Why, I ask, should that be so? Why are laws so precise that creative scientists can engineer Rosetta's landing of Philae on a distant comet after ten years of space travel?

Suppose we could make laws flexible, to be always beneficial, never painful. So when convenient, gravity is suspended to prevent crash landings; hard solid objects become soft liquids, so glass never cuts on impact, collapsing concrete buildings turn to powder, and bullets melt; electricity gives lighting but never lightning strikes; rain grows crops but never drowns. Would such unpredictable, irregular 'laws' and unstable environment be an improvement on the present? Isn't fixity better than flux, making it advantageous when cause and effect operate regularly, so a sharp knife, lethal gun and drunken driver are always dangerous?

Thereby, people can predict outcomes more reliably and use God's gift of freewill to act more responsibly for good or ill. It is also fairer as we all have to play in an independent environment by the same rules, not bending them to suit ourselves and have special weather, harvests, or immunity from disease.

Having proposed a better world through three alterations, to our liberty, comfort, and laws, I now need to ask a crucial question: "Would I be there to enjoy my improvements?" No! The present 'me' would not exist! Inadvertently I have committed suicide! My re-tuning of the world would alter the whole package. Indeed, without fixed laws, would *any* universe be possible and would it contain *any* life? Whatever creatures existed would be weird aliens, probably unable to grumble and propose further changes!

Why not a fourth 'improvement', no death? Accepting that the birth and death of stars was necessary to give us birth, I might have wanted life, as soon as it emerged, to escape that cycle, so I would never age and die! Again, that would be suicidal. It was the death of dinosaurs that provided opportunities for other species to arrive, including humans! We are told that nearly all past species have died out, with beneficial effects - I assume - on present species. Human progress 'stands on the shoulders' of previous generations, so flora and fauna progress may well do the same.

When we are heartbroken at the death of our loved ones, we may wish that they and we could live on, unseparated. But our survival would be at the expense of future generations. Finite resources on a crowded planet cannot sustain an infinite number of lives. My death and recycled body makes room for others. Again, my 'improvement' lets me down!

# Hindu, Buddhist, Muslim and Christian ideas about suffering

My emphasis has been on Christianity, partly because suffering is the heart of the matter. But other religions confront it too. Their followers also offer Mayday distress prayers that often fail to work miracles and produce the desired outcome. The God of the Jews in Nazi concentration camps did not rescue them as they believe he did in the exodus from Egypt over 3000 years ago. The hands of a typically non-interventionist God are those of caring families and professionals, all keen to alleviate pain, though earlier pain may have helped the diagnosis. So I now turn to look briefly at how three other religions offer hope in the midst of suffering.

Hinduism is more a collection of divergent beliefs rather than one orthodox creed. Ancient Vedas (1500-500 BC), and later Upanishads, and Bhagavad Gita, include many deities and rituals, but also witness to a single divine reality. Among the gods and goddesses are Brahma (the creator), Vishnu (the preserver), and an 'opposing' Shiva (the destroyer). But these may be different ways of conceiving one reality behind all things, Brahman, the spiritual essence of the universe. At the core of each human being (*atman*), is a trace of this ultimate reality and this unchanging atman is the permanent link between successive rebirths.

In Hinduism a person's enduring soul transmigrates in rebirth, like a baton passed on in a relay race. One's karma (action) has good or evil consequences, happiness or misfortune: each individual is both the cause of his own suffering and his own potential saviour by liberating himself from the cycle of births and deaths, allowing the sage to become merged into, not nothingness, but the divine and ultimate existence at the heart of the universe.

Buddhists have many pagodas and personal shrines where they can honour Buddha, give offerings, pray for help, and kneel in respect and reverence, if not worship. The purists in Theravada Buddhism see it as more of a moral philosophy than a religion. Original Buddhism, without a Creator-God to worship, focuses on personal spiritual development. Buddha, Siddhartha Gautama, went on a quest for Enlightenment around the sixth century BC and finally reached *nirvana*. This 'awakened one' was like a physician, diagnosing suffering that is endemic in all forms of life as the cause of our troubles, and proposing its cure through detachment from desire, and mind-control of unstable emotions. He realised that everything is impermanent: our mistaken belief that things can last is a chief cause of suffering. Unlike Hindu continuity of the soul, the Buddhist has no fixed self but a changing ego, so what lives on after death - as a result of karma's cause and effect - is the accumulating product of what has been done before death and in previous lives.

Through the practice of morality and meditation, all Buddhists follow the Eightfold path or Middle Way of the Buddha that avoids the extremes of indulgence and asceticism. The goal is nirvana; liberation that Buddha showed is possible in one lifetime, the culmination of a cycle of his reincarnated lives. That nirvana means extinguishing, putting out the fires of greed and desire, and release from suffering, in a new peaceful, blissful state of mind, with compassion for all living things.

Allah is the Arabic name for God that Muslims use. Muhammad (peace be upon him) is his final prophet, 570-632 AD, to whom the sacred Word of God, the Qur'an, was revealed. It teaches that Allah is a Unity, One who created everything and also sustains all creation in being, moment by moment. He is the Greatest, who rules over all and submission to his supreme will is crucial, especially in the face of suffering which can test, punish, and purify his followers. He is the source of both good and evil though the Qur'an also assumes some moral responsibility in humans. Allah is the most Merciful, so whom he wills he forgives.

Obedience is central to the disciplined life of Muslims, in their practice of its Five Pillars, five obligations to recite the creed, pray five times daily, to fast, give alms, and make a pilgrimage to Mecca. The faithfulness of all human beings will be assessed on the Day of Judgement by Allah who rewards and punishes fairly. Though their destiny is already known by omniscient Allah, there is sufficient choice in life for people to become worthy of entering heaven and avoiding the suffering in hell.

My readers will reach their own conclusions on how these three religions - in so far as my inadequate summary allows - throw light on the problem of suffering. They point, in my view, in the right direction by seeking to reduce some suffering by employing more spiritual resources than material. A tsunami cannot be controlled whereas some mind-control and inward serenity is possible in Buddhism's sensible detachment from desire and possessions. I respect the sense of brotherhood amongst Muslims, and their call to make daily devotions the spine of daily life not the fingernail, to stand tall even in times of hardship and suffering. I am not distracted by the many gods and ritualism in Hinduism because it points me to a more sophisticated meaning and unity beyond them, accessible through meditation. The advocates of karma are aware that it does not properly solve why the *innocent* suffer, often through natural disasters, or through their intended good deeds turning out to have bad or unforeseeable consequences. My view of the soul as not a box put into a body, but a growing up process, of increasing self-awareness, wisdom, and spirituality, overlaps a little with the Buddhist idea of a changing self.

My chief challenge to believers in all religions is this: *how do you know* that underlying reality, God, Yahweh, Allah, Brahman, or whatever is good? What makes you so certain? Is belief in their goodness based on evidence that holds water? Or is it based on collective faith that may be more of a leap in the darkness of our suffering world?

Christianity claims - arrogantly it may seem to outsiders - to know the answer. It alone pins its hope on a historical event as the best defence against God's alleged inhumanity. Unlike Vishnu's ten incarnations known as avatars, there was one supremely shocking divine intervention 2000 years ago. It made tangible the philosopher's God in 'My First Assumption', by embodying a suffering God, who in Jesus shared our dangers. From Bethlehem baby to carpenter and teacher he was vulnerable to sickness, cuts from chisels, and physical abuse, in a remarkable combination of weakness and power. Confronted by a man born blind, Jesus denied that sin had caused the blindness and by healing him he showed God's wish for the man's wholeness (13).

But though his miracles helped others, Jesus did not ask for them to save himself. Crucified, he forgave his killers, and felt "forsaken" by his Father God who did not intervene. The Almighty let it happen - as I have

argued throughout - from Big Bang creation to cruci-
fixion, Power restrained itself. Remove the cross and
*any belief* in a compassionate God becomes harder to
justify. Remove the unique resurrection of Jesus whom
God raised with 'earth-shattering' power, and
Christianity loses its best reason for believing in the
eventual defeat of evil and suffering.

To explain how a painful cross could be compatible
with a compassionate God would lengthen this little
book, so may I refer you to CC instead? There I also
examine the evidence for the resurrection of Jesus and
debate whether it was physical or spiritual. But either
way, Christianity claims it has a credible hope, based
on sufficient evidence that underlying reality is good,
on our side (14).

# God's absence or presence alongside

The same Father God who let Jesus die for us, may also not intervene to stop a child or teenager dying from cancer or - in our grandson's case - stop his seizures. All distressed parents may, like Jesus, feel God-forsaken, abandoned to do the best they can in the situation, when their prayers hit the ceiling. Though no *super-natural* help may arrive, what often arrives is the *natural* practical support of family and friends. Regularly, BBC Children in Need raises many millions and its television presenters rightly thank the public for their generosity. Similarly, when television pictures show harrowing scenes following a tsunami wave, another counteracting wave of worldwide generosity follows and survivors bounce back with enormous resilience to repair the damage (not only, I suspect, due to the genes mentioned p38). Who knows how much of this wellspring of human goodness is God-inspired and merits our prayers of thanksgiving? (15)

Some reassurance may come to the child or teenager's parents by the thought that God sees their child's cancer as a tragic accident, an unforeseeable malfunction of cells, and an agonising frustration of his wish for the child's and teenager's long, joyful life. Nothing was fated or destined to happen. Rather, it is natural processes that can undermine his good wishes and make life precarious. If we measure the unwavering love of God only by evidence of remissions, successful operations or chemotherapy, a believer's faith may wobble, despite knowing that earthly bodies are unsafe, and the soul's only security is in God's eternity.

A wobbling parent brought his demon-possessed epileptic son to Jesus for healing and cried "I believe; help my unbelief" (16). More convinced parents may discover that God had no *purpose for* the crisis but once it arrived he has a redeeming *purpose in it, attempting* to bring a positive out of the most negative situation. God can have spiritual influence on events he chooses not to control, to bring out the best in people, and help them live with or survive the nightmare. "God's influence most on minds and hearts/ Through prayer forgives, mends attitudes/ Such healing of the mind may help/ The body's battle with disease" (17).

Some fortunate parents and their children may feel held by a pain-sharing God in Christ, whose cross is an everlasting divine memory. That sharing God knows the sufferers by name and loves them as much if not more than we do. Believe it or not, he promises to be alongside, 'under the rubble' with the crushed children in a bombed classroom. On an excruciating cross, Jesus requested his Father to forgive his executioners and we can imagine the Father's merciful response (18).

But I hope it is not blasphemy or irreverent to

wonder if the Father also had a request: "Humans, forgive me for the way things had to be, for unavoidable death, disease and disasters". If that is true, forgiveness could become mutual. We know the Lord's Prayer says "Forgive us the wrong we have done, as we have forgiven those who have wronged us" (19). There can be God's mercy for our sin, and those sufferers who feel they have been immensely wronged may in time be able to pardon and accept the Creator's world. That exchange may bring a little peace, a feeling of not just resignation and submission, but reconciliation, a spiritual healing of our anger and protests.

We might expect omniscient God to be all-knowing, not at all unknowing. But I have already suggested he knows only all that is possible to know, not next year's deaths from avalanches, terrorism, lightning, or in childbirth. God created not evil but the *possibility* of evil by knowingly starting and permitting the evolution of a global system whose outcome would result in unquantified suffering and disease. He could not know in advance your family tragedy nor did he plan, will, allow, sanction or permit it before it happened.

Nor does God tolerate your heartache, in the sense of doing nothing about it, for he works intolerantly to try to overcome evil with good, if he can. But 'tolerate' also has the dictionary sense of 'to suffer to be done', to 'bear', to 'endure', and those words came true on the cross, so in that sense we might say God tolerates his global package, because the gains outweigh the losses and inevitable heartaches it causes.

# Miracles of two sorts

I distinguish between what I call *'co-natural* miracles' and *'supernatural* miracles'. The former may be more common than we realise, as God works along the grain of his natural laws - not suspending them - to produce 'miraculous' recoveries. Mystified doctors might prefer to call them 'inexplicable', or coincidences of timing, rather than Godincidences. In contrast, the "typically non-interventionist God" that I have described makes *supernatural* miracles rare occurrences. He does not set aside known laws, to enable a windfall apple to rise conveniently into my open hand! God can be trusted to let all nature run its course, maintaining an inflexible law of gravity of benefit to us all.

Indeed, the supreme miracle on which Christianity depends, God raising Jesus from the dead, may not be a *suspension* of known physical laws but God's temporary supernatural *superimposition* of other natural phenomena - as yet unknown to science - to *transform* a dead body. That defies our common sense but current scientific knowledge also admits to some weird, nonsensical aspects of quantum mechanics, dark matter and dark energy.

A temporary superimposition suggests that Jesus was an exceptional case, as Christians believe. The incarnation means that Jesus was the fullest possible expression of God-on-Earth without threatening his humanity. So his death was a real death but his resurrection was God's unique doing. In that light, such selectivity is understandable, however incredible it may seem.

Co-natural miracles are problematic. Why does a good God sometimes tip the natural scales in favour of a few rather than always for everyone? Some believers get remissions, others don't. That appears arbitrary and unfairly immoral of a good God. I have no answer to that, other than to rule out all co-natural miracles, and to refer you back to the resilience comments (p38).

But I have no right or desire to rule out the evidence of other people's experience and at the same time to limit God's freedom more than he may wish. To the believer in miracles, faith-healing does occur as God takes advantage of the immense possibilities in the subatomic quantum world to do the unexpected. It is a believer's faith that turns events into a miracle but nobody can be certain that one occurred and prayers were answered in the way desired.

# Reunions in heaven - are they possible?

At funerals, it is consoling to think of death as a gateway and of being eventually reunited to those we love. We want jam tomorrow if we can't have it today! Some critics of religion think it offers pie in the sky only when we die!

Though Jesus spoke of future togetherness, he did dampen expectations of sexual bodies in heaven - unlike the sensual paradise that the Qur'an declares. When Jesus was asked about reunions for separated couples, here is his reported realism: "When they rise from the dead, men and women do not marry; they are like angels in heaven". So there is discontinuity between bodies now and whatever identity and reunion one has in eternity. But there will be continuity of my 'essence' - Mary gradually recognised the resurrected, *transformed* Jesus (20).

More than that is beyond us. We do not know *what* happens, yet faith knows *who* welcomes us, into a spiritual heaven - surely not a place - where God is the centre, not our wishes. With him, all will be well, so I finished my *CC* dedication to my grandchildren with "to Daniel in gratitude for what he has given me and in the hope he will ultimately be complete with God".

# A summary in seven sentences

I shall now over-simplify by reducing my argument to just seven steps, which the Appendix will expand into twenty two. All the steps are in sequence so each one is the result of what precedes it:

- God exists and acts according to his perfectly good nature.
- He chooses to give freedom to creation, and restrict his own power.
- An apparently self-governing universe - sustained by God - evolves as a violent package.
- Our changing Earth has the hallmarks of that package.
- Earth's creatures experience both pleasure and pain without God's interventions.
- Humans multiply God's virtues but more funda- mental improvements to the world's foundations would fail to make life better.
- Religious faith maintains hope now and beyond.

That hope will be developed in the conclusion. These seven steps may imply that the universe is more human-centred than the evidence allows, and more than some advocates of the anthropic principle would like (21). Earth is a minor planet orbiting an average star amongst billions in our galaxy added to billions of galaxies. Their meaning and purpose are beyond me but I assume that the whole universe - and possible multiverse - have value in their own right, not just for human benefit.

Are humans unique? Geneticists line up the DNA sequence of different mammalian species and only a keen eye, or better a computer, can spot the very small differences across most of the genome. But though 98% of our DNA is the same as a chimpanzee's, our *significance* is not just 2% more than a chimpanzee (nor twice as much as a banana); we are 100% human beings! In my view they have become a special creation (uplifted by God, though I cannot prove it, nor can the atheist prove his absence!). A small variation, especially in language, can make a gigantic difference in their unique significance. Current knowledge makes human understanding unique: no other animal can understand the laws of the universe, as if it - or the Creator - "knew we were coming" (22).

But human suffering is not unique in nature's Darwinian world. Animal pain is a controversial area that would expand my book. All I will say is that I have seen distressed animals in an abattoir queue, bellowing *in advance*, whereas we humans can foresee our own, possibly painful end, years ahead.

# Earth, the optimum, or only possible world

Einstein remarked to his assistant Ernst Straus, "What really interests me is whether God could have created the world any differently; in other words, whether the demand for logical simplicity leaves any freedom at all" (23). Probably, the universe has the properties we observe because no other universe is possible, it is the only recipe nature allows.

Alternatively, before the Big Bang, the greatest Mind may have compromised, balancing gains and losses between possible alternatives in his fertile imagination, to find the optimum for his goal of Good. We inhabit either the only possible world or the only optimal world to achieve his loving purposes, despite the suffering involved. Either way, this imperfect world is God's unfinished business, a work in progress that is more dynamic than Leibniz could know.

I have ended up attaching new meaning to the idiom 'There is no place like home'. Despite the agony and ecstasy in our turbulent world, it is still our best home. Whether or not there is an afterlife, the importance of the Earth remains unchanged: contrary to what some preachers suggest, believers and unbelievers are all in the same boat! Earth is still the only home all of us shall ever have with our *present bodies and minds*. So this life is not a rehearsal but the one and only performance. It would be short-sighted to devalue Earth into simply a waiting room for the hereafter. All that any of us can do is to make the most of the present moment, nowness, and make a difference to where we are.

Where does that leave the afterlife? Though the Jewish scriptures say relatively little about it, it is there in some form or other in all religions, as part of the meaning of our lives. For me, meaning, purpose, and greater human happiness are rooted in all virtues, especially in love and forgiveness.

However, will the love given and received between family, friends, and the strangers helped through our charitable outreach, outlast us? The pessimist might say it lasts only so long as those survivors themselves remember and survive. My optimistic view is that like energy, it cannot be lost, but is somehow passed on, accumulated, not simply a microscopic addition to humanity's 'metaphorical DNA' - or Richard Dawkins' meme, an inherited cultural idea - but given eternal value by the One who is its ultimate source and whose universal love seeks to embrace all. Belief in that eternal value would be extremely shaky without the evidence I have already alluded to in the cross and resurrection of Jesus, that are the turning points in human history (24).

A person approaching death could say to himself: "If God is Good, Holy Love, and my heavenly Father who loves me now, is he likely to want to scrap tomorrow what matters to him now?"

With God, there is an eternity of infinite possibilities, in his open 'home', that excludes present evil. There he will mercifully "wipe every tear from their eyes, death will be no more, mourning and crying and pain will be no more, for the first things have passed away" (25). Reading that, those in the heat of battle, facing death or caring for the long-term sick or dying, may find that trite words like 'consolation' or 'compensation in religion' fail to express what they feel. Nevertheless, the Christian hope gives God the benefit of the doubt, and trusts him to bring an end to grief and injustice, when the unending future will make more meaning and sense of the past (26).

Space explorations may modify my conclusion. We cannot rule out the possibility of life on other planets and even - unlikely as it may seem - a better, populated world elsewhere. But meanwhile we, as God's stewards, are tasked with not ruining our changing planet with its evolving humans, thereby frustrating his local intentions.

# God's equation

Einstein gave us $E = mc^2$.
Energy = mass x the speed of light squared.

But that was God's equation many billions of years before Einstein discovered it. From what I have written, it appears that the God of Energy also had in mind a non-mathematical version of the same equation.

$E = mc^2$ is his purposeful process.
Evolution brings Morality and Creativity but at a much slower, painstaking speed. That pain includes unavoidable suffering.

# Appendix: A simplification in 22 steps

to help your private study or group discussion of
*Suffering: if God exists, why doesn't he stop it?*

1. A Creator-God exists as an idea and assumed reality.
2. He is Good by nature and choice, the greatest conceivable goodness.
3. God's moral nature gives him moral purpose to multiply his goodness.
4. He is Love which is the greatest Good, wanting everything else to reach its best potential.
5. God is ethical perfection, a holy love that seeks to reform the imperfect.
6. Omnipotent God chooses to restrict his power to fit his purpose.
7. His Big Bang gave freedom to matter and life to evolve and make itself, sustained by God.
8. A fixed plan gives no freedom to a Discoverer God nor to his creatures.
9. Freedom has to be in both people and their stardust particles.
10. Creative God relinquishes control to endow creativity on his creation.
11. That entails success and failure, beneficial mutations and disabilities.
12. Robots would be worthless, unable to choose to be

good.

13. Moral virtues grow through hard choices in agonising situations.

14. Suffering is part of the package, the unavoidable consequence.

15. God aims to make good beings in his image, freely responding to his love and multiplying it to others.

16. The ambiguous means to that end bring big gains and sad losses in natural disasters and human evil.

17. Rough justice is inevitable if virtue is to be chosen for its own sake.

18. Improvements to the world would be no good to us and defeat God's purpose.

19. Compared with other religions, only Christianity has a suffering God.

20. Jesus shared our pain and felt God-forsaken. His resurrection is the first fruit of eventual victory over evil.

21. God is alongside, influencing open minds and willing hearts, to help them cope.

22. God will eventually achieve his moral purpose and all will be well.

# References

1. p18 CC.
2. p47 CC.
3. *Isaiah* 55:8. "God moves in a mysterious way/his wonders to perform" is a William Cowper hymn. It was Leibniz who asked "Why is there something rather than nothing?"
4. *Ps.* 103:6, 145:17; *Gen.* 18:25; *Lev.* 19:2; *Isaiah* 6.
5. *Gen.* 1:27.
6. Stephen Hawking and Leonard Mlodinow: *The Grand Design*, 2011; Martin Rees: *Just Six Numbers*, 2001; Lawrence Krauss: *A Universe from Nothing*, 2012.
7. Paul Davies: *The Mind of God*, 1992; Fred Hoyle: *The Intelligent Universe*, 1983.
8. John Polkinghorne: *Science and Religion in Quest of Truth*, 2011; *The Boyle Lectures: Science and Religion in Dialog*ue, 8 April 2013.
9. Freeman Dyson thinks "the capacity to make choices, is to some extent inherent in every electron" in Ervin Laslo: *Science of the Akashic Field - an Integral Theory of Everything*, (2004) p148.
10. *1 John* 4:7-21. George Herbert's poem, *Love (III)*, has the Love of God as a waiter serving his guests.
11. *Matt.* 5:45. These non-automatic moral ripples might be contrasted with the Big Bang ripples, detected as recently as 1965, in the form of cosmic

microwave background radiation, equally distributed in the observable sky.

12. Jennifer Couzin-Frankel, *"The bad luck of cancer"*, *Science*, 2 Jan. 2015, Vol. 347, no. 6217, on research by Vogelstein & Tomasetti, John Hopkins University, showing many cases of cancer are not preventable.

13. *John* 9. It was customary then to blame Satan or demon possession for illness, *Luke* 13: 16; *Job* 2:4-7. The Lord's Prayer mentions "the evil one" who tempted Jesus in the wilderness, *Matt.* 6:13; 4:1-11. For the power or power-emptying of Jesus, see *Phil.* 2: 6-11.

14. For a contemporary idea of how Jesus's death on the cross saved us, bringing 'atonement', see *CC* pp 105-128. All the evidence for Christ's physical or spiritual resurrection is listed and debated on pp130-139 *CC*. All religions teach what humans must *do*, but only Christianity adds what God *has done*. All ask for human effort, whereas Christianity adds God's effort and provision. This is paradoxical: Jesus calls for the highest ethical attainment, but he also does for us what we cannot do for ourselves!

15. A Jewish prophet thought otherwise: "It was I who brought starvation," *Amos* 4:6; *Isaiah* 53:4. Old Testament writers sometimes attributed to God what today we would explain differently. Instead

of writing a chain of causes, their shorthand made God the ultimate cause of blessing and punishment, *Deut.* 28; *Isaiah* 40:2; *Ez.* 18. For today's view of God's responsibility, and causes, see *CC* pp26-27, 45-51.

16. *Mark* 9:24.

17. *CC* pp178-183; *Rom.* 8:26-28.

18. That "divine memory" presumably includes the wounded - can one say disabled? - hands and feet of the risen Jesus, that he invited his frightened disciples to inspect and touch, *Luke* 24:36-39. *The Disabled God* is a Nancy Eiesland title and as a disabled person she wanted her lifelong disability that formed her identity to accompany her into eternity. I am at a loss to see how that could be possible in a non-physical heaven. Yet I have argued throughout that God chose to 'disable' himself metaphorically by restricting his own power to intervene in order to give freedom to his creation. *Heb.* 2:10-18, 4:14-16; 1 *Cor.* 10:13.

19. *Matt.* 6:12.

20. *Mark* 12:18-27; *John* 20:1-18.

21. See Richard Feynman in James Gleick: *Genius: Richard Feynman and Modern Physics*, 1994.

22. Freeman Dyson in John Barrow and Frank Tipler: *The Anthropic Cosmological Principle*, 1986.

23. Albert Einstein: Quoted by Ernst Straus in Carl Seelig: *Helle Zeit - Dunkle Zeit*, 1956.

24. Compare Virgil: *"Omnia vincit Amor"*, Love conquers all, *Eclogues* (37BC); W.H. Auden: *"We must love one another or die"*, *1 September, 1939*; Philip Larkin: *"What will survive of us is love"*, *An Arundel Tomb*. But both Larkin and Auden later regretted their lines.

25. *Rev.* 21:4; "universe...groans as if in childbirth", *Rom.* 8:18-39, *Revised English Bible*, the version used for all my references which are not used as definitive proof texts to settle an argument. One reference has to be balanced against another, and the context is always important.

26. My "sense of the past" is cautious compared with writers who promise a future heavenly tapestry or embroidery, with its neat pattern on one side, which results in the other side's disorder and Earthly mess. This analogy, however comforting, may also mislead sufferers to think that all Earth's painful criss-cross needlework in their lives was knowingly planned and purposed by the designer to make his predetermined pattern, omitting the chance and designer's frustration I described on p29. Hopefully, heaven's compensation will reveal a redemptive *overall* pattern that *finally emerges* triumphant, and specially rewards the unlucky on Earth.

    See *CC* pp114-117, 198-208 for ideas about heaven and hell, the Last Judgement, and the victory of forgiveness over our failures (grace over law). This End is really a new beginning, more universal than the promised Second Coming of Jesus to Earth. That coming, whether literal or figurative, symbolises the ultimate victory of Good when the panoramic rule of God will be cosmic, not parochial. Any earthly rule of humans on this temporary planet would not change the plight of its other suffering creatures or the natural disasters built into its revolutions around a sun that in a few billion years will run out of fuel.

# A surgeon's view

*When I look at the hand - an amazingly complex structure which underpins all we think and do - I sometimes wonder whether it really could have evolved by chance into this perfect piece of engineering or whether somewhere along the line it was designed.*

*As a hand surgeon I face every day the paradox between spirituality and science that John Morris addresses in his wonderful book. Each patient tells me how the problem in their hand affects their hobbies, happiness, work, ambition, family obligations; they confide their fears and hopes. I am privileged to have them let me so deeply and openly into their soul, their personality, their humanity. But then to treat them I have to revert to being a scientist- I have to work out exactly what has happened to their anatomy, mechanics and biochemistry.*

*So are we just chemical reactions, biological processes, mechanical machines? If my patient's medical problem is merely a physical aberration, why does it impart such a human effect that manifestly transcends the science of the hand. And the more I realise that, the more I realise that to treat the whole patient I have to treat the human being, not just the human structure.*

*Morris's book, rationalising science with the soul, allowing design yet evolution and anomaly, gives me more insight into this most fundamental conflict and will, I hope,*

*make me a better doctor.*
**Professor David Warwick,** Hand Surgeon, Faculty of Medicine, University of Southampton

*This is a very valuable book. The subject of suffering has exercised the greatest of human minds and challenged all who believe in a benevolent creator God. Yet the mystery remains, though it has proved possible to explore some of its depths helpfully. John Morris has condensed his work into a mere 68 pages without dodging the most difficult questions and without being superficial. Like all the best theology, it is personal, and unlike much theology it is expressed in vigorous, direct language accessible to the thoughtful lay mind. It is a remarkable achievement for which many will be very grateful.*
**Very Revd Trevor Beeson,** Dean Emeritus of Winchester Cathedral

*A handy and helpful introduction to the many issues that need to be taken into account before one can arrive at a considered response to the question raised.*
**Russell Stannard, OBE,** Emeritus Professor of Physics, Open University

*Morris uses a unique blend of science, philosophy, scripture and personal experience to give a well-considered response to the age-old question 'Why does God allow suffering?' God seems to have paid a price in setting up the laws of the*

*universe in that He doesn't appear to break them very frequently. Hence, suffering is introduced. Could there have been any other way? An excellent read. You will be hooked.*
**Dr James R. Smith,** Senior Research Fellow, School of Pharmacy and Biomedical Sciences, University of Portsmouth

*This book is a brave shot at what is probably impossible - to know or explain the mind of God. In the process, it is full of fascinating insights - into scripture, science, human nature and the meaning of the apparently simple word 'good'.*
**Canon David Winter,** former Head of BBC Religious Broadcasting

*John Morris's book is an excellent opportunity for students to explore the issues that arise from the extremely contentious issue of evil and suffering. Its clear and concise style makes it an ideal companion to all A Level syllabi but would also be suitable for able GCSE students with an interest beyond the syllabus. I wholeheartedly recommend it.*
**Richard Harvey,** Head of Religious Studies, Harrow School, Harrow on the Hill

*John Morris presents a clear and rational approach to the question of how a loving God 'allows' suffering. His focus on the big picture, using a systematic approach drawing on science, leads to the conclusion that God has created the best possible world for the evolution of morality and creativity.*

*He provides a refreshingly logical and helpful framework in which to understand God, his creation and the inevitability of suffering.*

**Jenny Nockolds,** Senior IT Project Manager, IBM, retired

*Belief in God can be hard at times, especially when we think about the suffering and evil in the world. Morris writes in a way that is sensitive, intelligent and immensely helpful, making faith in God more credible and more possible. This is a book I shall read again and again.*

**Rt Revd Peter Hancock,** Bishop of Bath and Wells, scientist

**Circle Books**

Circle is a symbol of infinity and unity. It's part of a growing list of imprints, including o-books.net and zero-books.net.

Circle Books aims to publish books in Christian spirituality that are fresh, accessible, and stimulating.

Our books are available in all good English language bookstores worldwide. If you can't find the book on the shelves, then ask your bookstore to order it for you, quoting the ISBN and title. Or, you can order online—all major online retail sites carry our titles.

To see our list of titles, please view www.Circle-Books.com, growing by 80 titles per year.

Authors can learn more about our proposal process by going to our website and clicking on Your Company > Submissions.

We define Christian spirituality as the relationship between the self and its sense of the transcendent or sacred, which issues in literary and artistic expression, community, social activism, and practices. A wide range of disciplines within the field of religious studies can be called upon, including history, narrative studies, philosophy, theology, sociology, and psychology. Interfaith in approach, Circle Books fosters creative dialogue with non-Christian traditions.

And tune into MySpiritRadio.com for our book review radio show, hosted by June-Elleni Laine, where you can listen to authors discussing their books.

MySpiritRadio